CONTOUR FEATHERS

POEMS
BY KEN HADA

Cover Painting:
Sometimes All We Have is Ourselves
© 2015 Sarah A. Hada
sarahhada.com

Book Design: Rowan Kehn

Turning Plow Press
www.turningplowpress.com

ACKNOWLEDGMENTS

I am grateful to the editors of the following journals, zines, and anthologies, in whose pages some of these poems first appear:

Arts Alive San Antonio, Delta Poetry Review, Depot TV // Norman Performing Arts Studio, Dragon Poetry Review, I-70 Review, Madness Muse Press, NonDoc.com, Open Windows Podcast, Poetica Review, San Pedro River Review, Sin Fronteras//Writers Without Borders, Stone Renga, Wordfest Anthology//Waco Cultural Arts Festival

Twelve poems in this collection were originally included in an electronic chapbook, titled *Contour Feathers*. The E-chapbook has been discontinued and the remaining poems have been collected in *Bring an Extry Mule* (Vacpoetry, 2017).

Contour Feathers, as an E-chapbook, was originally dedicated to Olga and Elida, two wonderful former students, who remain dedicated professional ladies and great friends.

I am especially grateful to Paul Bowers who was a first reader and thoughtful editor of many of these poems. I also remain grateful for my brother, Alan Berecka, who always understands.

for Roxie Faulkner Kirk

a near perfect cousin
and husband Terry
who helps us keep it between the ditches

and

Gary Worth Moody

whose generosity is boundless

TABLE OF CONTENTS

THE TENUOUS FRAGILITY OF NOW

After a Shock

I'm trying to get back
to normal, but
there is no normal
to get back to.

We have it so good,
thus we are in peril.
We are afraid
of what we fear to fear.

Grief

is mysteriously ordinary
but always individual.

It can be nothing else.

It is a leafless tree
despite April sun.

It is a bite
of overbaked birthday cake –
the sweetness burnt
into bitter crust.

No one can taste
for you.

Your destiny
(like those standing around)
is to swallow,
grimace,
then smile.

By God,
you'd better smile.

An Osprey

circles the brassy water,
loops two, three times
or more, drops
a few hundred feet,
flaps his shimmering wings
in white afternoon sun,
climbs, repositions,
then plummets
like a terrible dagger
splashing the edge of water
to claim his prey,
piercing the flesh
of a fish lucky enough
never to know the force
that guarantees survival.

Asymptomatic

What death we carry
within us, without
a trace, no sign
to suspect complicity.

What death we convey
to those who trust us.
Foggy mornings
obscure the truth of the sun.

Betrayal of our bodies
is but surface –
what hides within
is our evil twin.

My Lilac

I have loved lilacs
ever since I was a boy
                    – Jonas Zdanys

I too had a Lilac when I was a boy.
The annual return of purple flowers
with divine fragrance in the April Ozarks
transfixed me – offered a presence,
a mystical experience I could not resist,
in ways I could not understand.

I was an ignorant mystic.
I see now that mysticism is felt,
something for the heart as much as
for the head – a phenomenon
that invokes enchantment,
pure in its simple complexity.

That fully-flowered bush entranced
this solitary, trusting, baseball-playing,
catfishing, muddy boot-wearing,
Bible-believing boy – made me pause
all activity, ponder the unknowable
every time I came close.

That bush initiated me into a way
of life – made me a disciple, following
a path of beauty – tender, fragrant –
gave me something else to believe in,
something I could touch, breathe –
behold in humble boyhood wonder.

Beside a white-piped clothesline, midst
towering walnut, hickory, and oak,
that flaming bush, sacred as any cross,
imprinted my soul for life – an image
I still follow – a fadeless impression
I have never been able to replicate.

Woodpecker

I hear his staccato bit
against a hidden tree trunk
somewhere over there,
some oak north and west
of where I sit in morning light
before humidity and wind
rise to obscure reception,
that sense of belonging
felt best in the stillness
in something we call soul
where everything common
fashions our moments
in meticulous repetition
of the marvelous unseen.

The Impulse to Respond

Tonight the moon wears a halo
the size of a small universe.

Some clichés are worth repeating,
the way we hear old symphonies anew,
as if we are in the composer's mind.
But it's not simply intellectual, is it?

The impulse to respond
to something beyond description
bears its own universality,
and I have nothing better to do
than watch night sky bursting in flames,
grateful that the ghosts about us
consider our dusty souls.

Missouri Evening Primrose

In June, these wild flowers bloom.
Evening nears. We assemble lawn chairs
semi-circle before the plant.
Bright yellow flowers to be unveiled
with the arrival of darkness.

Expectation is palpable – we wait
excited to see the first flower
emerge from its protective green pod

like waiting on your friend's plane to land,
like a child traveling to grandma's for Christmas,
like your lover's phone call –

if you're not too dull to appreciate beauty,
or too busy or too jaded to embrace a shrub
bursting to life before your eyes.

It's still light – whippoorwills have not yet begun
to sing, a bat darts through heavy sky.
Sun settles slowly through hills of white oak.

Any moment now, the "Ozark Sun Drop"
will appear, will open, spread tender petals.

This night flower trades places with the sun,
as if to remind us life flourishes even in darkness.
Speechless, we watch the births of flowers.

The Creek at Night

for Kent & Beci

Soon darkness will be complete.
Only memory sounds through the night:
water trickles under a bluff
where streaks of pale light linger
the certainty of setting sun
filtered through darkening leaves.

Soon darkness will be everything,
the only thing – even now,
despite the illusion of light
painted on this rocky canvas
fragments of a life reflected
onto the clear water below.

Nothing is spared. All things hidden,
every known thing, gives way
to the dark. The best things last
but a minute before darkness comes.
But sounds of water remain.
The sound of water is never hushed.

Stones Unseen

Some stones unseen rest
like clouds becoming nothing
we have overlooked.

I have stubbed my toe
too often to remember
when the path was clear.

The harder I dig, the more
I discover what forms me.

Some stones unseen rest
while dreams of desire emerge
inexplicably

in cold silence – the hard truth
lingering timeless as rock.

Now the Rain

A few sprinkles
as I listen to sounds
of Mozart – or is it Brahms,
or some other master
on morning radio

grow louder by the moment.

Now the rain – dropping
with matchless rhythm
replaces the music of man
coming through a machine
connecting me to ages past.

Now the singing rain, as always,
crescendos, commands
everything – moves me
back to origins I cannot estimate.

I can always turn a radio
off and on. But rain,
in its undeterred, symphonic score,
with its primal surprises,
offers relief from summer sweat,
a reassessment of everything.

Pulse

The way early sun
behind cottonwoods
seeps a soft orange
glow, dusty –
like so many things
overlooked, misunderstood,
taken for granted.

Silent greens below,
upturned leaves
at tree-top,
all feel the same pulse
while a crow cackles,
and out there,
chickadees squeak like hinges.

Shadows

Shadows say more to me
than perhaps they should

but then again, a cup of coffee
has long been my best friend

and morning cries the tears
of the ambushed —

congressmen hawking trinkets
at the subway.

So I listen, try to hear
what shadows have to say

especially when the coffee
grinds to a close,

empty as the sole of a boot
scattered in the alley

behind Union Station, or
or windowless brick building

left for dead on a ruptured street
in small town Oklahoma

a once-upon-a-time tale,
greedy as neon, or the capitol

where betrayal and heroism foil
shadows of destiny.

Summer Night

A bullfrog croaking at pond's edge
like a trombone player
on stage, as if he owns the world.

Tonight, he does.
Tonight, he does.

June Haiku

A breeze like leather
pommels the prairie,
saddles white oak hills.

Blue clouds blow my way.
Rain taps the coarse prairie grass.
Yesterday softens.

Life is water
cutting a way through rock.
Be your own stream.

August Nights

When the sky is on fire,
your skin swelters
and you learn you
are rock, molten.

Looking up at rock
falling, your heart wells,
even June bugs
cannot deter your gaze

as if you will leave
all this organic stuff
grounding you, as if,
somehow, you should.

Chuck-Will's-Widow

Chanting like a holy man
with relentless energy
to conjure what we
have yet to understand

filling me with simultaneous
feelings of dread
and resolve.

I cannot ignore such an oracle.

I can only wonder
where the primitive energy
goes, how it exists
to begin with, and what
I am to do
with the mortal accident
of hearing

how to participate
with a private mystic
so forcefully present

like water flowing
in an unmarked stream,
like the constant glow
of a moon forever silent
all around us.

Listening to Sibelius

His *Concerto in D Minor for Violin*
and Orchestra soothes
through summer night
under a half-moon,
a soft breeze.

Tree frogs and Chuck-will's-widow
provide dissonant rhythm,
join this introspective score
where prairie and sky
come together at dusk.

Looking Up

I look up
to discover
in quiet surprise
ten vultures
circling
high above,
their dark shapes
cruising
cloudless blue sky,
wing tips silvered
in sun.

I watch them,
wonder what has died,
think about death,
then look away
to catch a breath.

I look up again,
watch them float away,
follow currents
higher than death,
higher than anything I know
about life.

September Woods

seem boundless,
a depth unknown –
a different darkness
than December

as if keeping secrets
is possible
before winter's
harsh unveiling.

Cedar Waxwings

They flood my trees.
But my camera cannot reach them.
No machine will conquer
this glory. Nothing
human controls this grace.

Each time I open the door
they scatter,
but some return.

I want to believe in returns
but I know some things
don't come back.

Today I am fortunate:
I ride an ecstatic tide watching
these gold-chested birds
perch with precise dignity,
erect, in the face of morning sun

not to replace what is forever gone

but to guide me
through the tenuous fragility
of Now.

THE DREAM WE DARE NOT DREAM

A Question Raised by Firelight

Destined by failure,
shaped by the rough cuts
of a dull blade

nonetheless, a hope
persists, a struggle
to believe

that belief has an end
worth all the effort.

If you think it is beautiful
then it must be

but is beauty
sufficient,
a worthy substitute
for what is lacking?

Moonlight Makes Its Way

A dark white, darker than purple cream,
but white against the night,

a moment of – what?
Hesitation? Omen? Fear?

I'm not sure. Not sure of myself.
Unsure of the world in which I find myself,
a universe closing in, finding me,
claiming me, with celestial paws.

I am a puppy lifted by the scruff of neck-fur,
held up for inspection.

Moonlight, now encroaching just above,
just beyond the tree-line of my closest horizon,
in silence – windless, even tree frogs
have gone quiet – moonlight
snailing through torpid sky –

harbinger of – what?
Death? Life?
forcing redefinition
of everything I think I know,
everything I think I am.

Dimensions

When morning sky is a frosty gray
so thick and opaque
you cannot discern dimensions,
you feel reduced to the clear truth,
diminished as you are.

You realize the undeniable fact
of your place in a gray overcast cosmos.
Anything else is temporary,
is but a pose – only the outlined forms
of birds or leafless branches
are knowable, no color is possible.

In the distance, you hear a faint call,
wonder how you appear,
what form you make to those
on the other side looking your way,
hard across eternal horizon.

When

When you can't feel the sun.

When you fail to notice the wind.

When you don't know how to pray
your way out of this, what to say
to implore goodness to overcome,
to spare us waste, hate and despair.

A field full of black cattle
goes on and on – never seems to end.
The yellow grass seems irrelevant,
inconsequential – just something
that happens to be around cattle.

When the lump in your throat
will not be swallowed

when the only dream
you've ever cared to dream
is not possible –

                too many things
make you
what you are not.

Landlocked

Sitting on a rocky overhang,
the Pacific waves, blue

and true, roll

beneath cloudless sky,

gulls aloft,
yellow flowers, green stems
at the mercy of wind
in my face, eyes
squinting
in salt-laced brightness.

I remember something
too easily forgotten,
flex my wings
into western wind,
rise in timorous flight.

I've been landlocked.

Here on this nameless point
of departure,
something stirs me,
frees me for journey,
makes flight possible.

The longer, the farther
I look, I realize what otherwise
could have been –

If only, like a gull
on recurring currents –
to be enjoyed
as much as envied.

In Your Wanting

Some solitude should not be resisted.
Outside my hut the river foams white,
rain dotting its silver surface,
blue clouds turning gray, swallow the basin.
Soon there will be no sky.

Trout can wait another time.
Even the heron knows to fold his wings,
duck into himself.

Now nothing but a river, rimming
with rain, offers reluctant
reassurance: In your wanting,
you are less than imagined,
but more than what you cannot have.

Beyond

Dying plants and candle
burned down to the wick

make me feel at home
the way a sliver of moon

slinks in a dark sky.
Every winged being

outside is free. Freedom
is out there, beyond

these brooding walls,
beyond the smell of wax.

The Beauty that Binds Us

Sunrise in our face,
my son and I drive
with silent determination
mixed with awe.

The beauty of morning
reflected inward
soothes like hot coffee
and a cinnamon roll.

Frustration escapes
every few miles,
the sense of loss
we both feel

familial betrayal
following us,
the politics of Jesus
arrogant as Nero.

We erupt, clear
our palates,
then renew quiet focus.
A trusted friend

morning sun,
streams bright rays
through dark clouds,
brightens the gloom.

We drive on. We will
not be consumed.
We will never betray
beauty that binds us.

Reclamation

I have nothing
but this rippling river
and a renewing
sense of self.

Sunlit water sparkles –
an inherited gift,
undeserved, splashing
unbending knees.

Wading this current,
rocks slippery underfoot,
flyrod arced
to divine today's truth.

Where else can a lost soul
reclaim something
misplaced – owning nothing,
receiving everything?

Incompletion

I beg God
for you to have redemption
I have never known.

Bargains are not much
better than begging
but groveling and grace
may be related.

If I am to be faithful
I must be
incomplete, waiting
to be completed,

but what is incompletion
but a recycled moment?

Like the seasons,
some days you see
what you are –
others, not.

Process is such cliché.
Journey is passé.

Yet I notice the sun
coming up
over the farthest hill.

A Place in the Woods

I walked the same way
each time I journeyed
into what then seemed deep
woods, submerging myself
beneath white oak, walnut
and so many other trees,
their limbs crisscrossing
to form an arc above me
where I sat between stones
matted soft with fallen leaves.

Settled in my spot
I would listen to wind,
to any sound around me.
I would look up at the arc,
through it, facing the sun
flickering from the other side.

I was too young to know
what meditation was;
I had only heard the word
worship, but something
like this must have been
happening to me,
something that drew me
back, finding my way
to a special place
where I would sit and wait
until I felt OK to return,
some release to emboldened
my steps toward home.

Redefinition

I feel the usual confliction –
anger, chagrin –

both offended
and offender,
both cause *and* effect.

What we know of history
offers so little hope.

Peace is a mirage.

Happiness rises and falls like dew
under moons that fall
through a dark cosmos

even as crows beat their wings
on unseen currents
above the oaks
standing close by.

But the oaks are not static.
The crow is not a monument.
Waves of motion
moving life, move me.

Self-consciousness drifts
between lonely self-immolation
and mis-placed assertion.

What are attempts at virtue worth?

Maybe the goal of arrival
is not the thing.

Maybe failed attempts
are the neutrons
of destiny.

Maybe destiny needs redefining.

Auditions

In darkness, sleep
writes a poem,
becomes the anthology
no one reads.

Hardback, collegial,
something to hold
in dumb wonder,
mimics days gone by.

Some things are true
but so much is chorus.
Auditions come
and I am un-costumed.

Who can help me?
Who will help me mask
to make some lines
of our own?

Hope, Temporary

At first it felt cautious,
like you weren't sure
how to walk on the ice,
how thick it was
above the water,
but then you believed
it was solid enough
to carry you
and you enjoyed
those safe moments
despite overhead sun.

But before long,
what you do not want to think about,
once again, becomes the deepest truth
you've always feared,
and the temporary stay of despair,
again, like perennial weeds,
like melting ice,
like anything recurrent,
becomes the thing
that undermines you –
the thing that digs your grave.

The Only One on Earth

Saturday morning rain absorbs all
I know for now. The winter grass.
The oaks remind me of nothing.
There is no one. No one else.
No governor and no two-bit
assistant who doesn't know poetry
from egg noodles. No Socrates.
No Cervantes. Faulkner vanishes.

The nightmare awakens me again.
The family pursuing me with passive
aggressive fervor, singling me out.
Cornering me in a sanctuary, then
in a house where I walk the halls
looking for any way out, or room
just to be safe, even if alone – anxiety
rising, trying to escape their virus,
their piety – false as ditch water
floating with cow shit after rain.

I am forced into ascetic virtue.
I would rather just be ordinary, but
nothing feels that way anymore.
I don't want to be a martyr.
I don't want to be a victim.
I just want to live in a country
where congress gives an ethical damn.

As long as that light flickers,
until that memory disappears,
I sing the solitude of self.
Alone – except for juncos and finches
in February – and an afternoon crow,
or two, sorting the ruins like jackals –
at least that is what I thought
when I saw them last.

Where do thoughts like that abide?
Who can know the heart?
(Go on, read the Old Testament!)
Not only is it deceitful, wicked
and unknowable, it is also weird.
Most especially, is it weird, strange,
confounding the self – looking
through a smudged glass
on a cloudy Saturday morning –
this, the only Saturday the world
has ever known.

Another Jay

Ok, I admit it:
You are beautiful.

Why God
made the ornery so striking
is beyond me.

At the bird bath,
like Narcissus,
you smugly gaze into a pool of water,
then preen away.

I want to believe in the common good,
in shared social acceptance
and mutual respect,
in just plain old decency

but the ways of the beautiful,
apparently,
can't be bothered.

The Sadness of Poets

I won't call it depression
though it may well be.
Call it sadness – a softer sound,
a subtle nuance – which poets prefer.

To play with words
is to play with the soul.
To organize worlds
when we know full well the chaos
bubbling below and about us
betrays that stage personae –
even the page is a white lie.

We see too much, know
just enough to be thought somewhat serious,
straggling an awkward dance
between the ultimate and the frivolous.

The gig's high only lasts a while
then we are brought down again
to the low-level of being
just ordinary.

Metaphors of time immemorial
stick to us like sandburs on socks –
the Sunday stroll in the park
turns into labor – and we
are unlucky leprechauns
lost in the weeds
wincing about magic.

We want to be read.
We want to be heard.
We want to be loved (at a respectable distance).
We want to be paid (without selling out).
We want to be happy (but stirred with melancholy empathy).

This is a sure sign you may be a poet:
You want what you can't have.
You want, and your wanting
is wasted on reconstruction.
Mortar-less bricks stand for a while,
look good, but rarely last.
The sadness of poets is softened by a reading
where other poets come together,
and we take turns being artist
and audience – our own agents
peddling ourselves to each other,
praying we may yet stand
when the bricks fall –
the never-built wall
always in need of repair.

So once more we enter the solace of solitude,
sharpen our simple tools,
wonder what comes next,
try not to think about a last gig.

Road Tripping

Road Work in Oklahoma City.
High wind warnings everywhere.

An island off an island
in the south Pacific seems as barren
now as it did when I saw those
black and purple volcanic nobs
poking up through stray grass
as I rode a lonesome bus
overcrowded with the human comedy

silent – like paintings hung
on a gallery wall – stories
all the same in their differing hues.

Food trucks in Texas –
brisket and most anything else you crave.

A man playing a broken horn
on the corner of State Street
in frozen Chicago.

Another rolls a cigar in New Orleans.
I stop to watch him work.
I pay my money
and walk through the Quarter
smoking the newness,
remembering how I got stuck
in traffic on Bourbon Street,
consider how I hate
just about all road work.

But that was yesterday.

Yesterdays are nothing.
Tomorrow is a vain dream.

Today, today, today creeps,
creeps, creeps –
this is the thing

even in Washington D C,
even in Moscow,
even at the mouth of a cave
in the Ouachita forest,
a place nobody would confuse
with the pursuit of happiness
or pledge allegiance.

It is the dream we dare not dream.

SEEKING MYSELF MORE THAN ANYTHING

On a Windless Summer Morning

On a windless summer morning
July's fragrance lingers
between the elm and oak,
sunflowers stand in line like schoolgirls
waiting their turn.

Without the wind
I am closer to my own breath.
I am full of bird energy
and flower pollen
coursing elastic veins.

What stillness does with a soul!
Absence of motion mirrors
secluded, latent motives, intent
on finding some meaning
in something.

Forward Looking

Trump flags are yet stiff
in awkward breeze –
plastic bags cling to barbwire.

Exes seem like granite.
You try to account for everything
done, everything undone.

You wonder if usual remedies
still apply – is forgiveness
really a thing? Is hope

only a mirage? You drive
across miles tortured
with anticipation – trying

to believe that motion
not only puts distance between
you and the past,

but also – Oh God, please –
that it is also taking
you somewhere.

When Christ Comes

after Carlos Fuentes
The Good Conscience

He arrives when I least expect him,
a vision, a childhood memory –
pure – before these days of compromise
when money and appearance rule
even private meditation.

Does the Christ of my childhood
expect my conflicted obedience
even now? How can I give away
what I have tried so hard to gain?
How can I lose what I save?

I once cleverly chimed:
If God is love, is love God?

Now this axiom seems self-serving,
as if I love, as if God doesn't see
through me to my hidden closet
filled with hurtful fretting –
fleecing anything resembling a cross.

The Nuthatch

works its way headfirst
down the trunk,
busy, unperturbed.

I receive this undertaking
with subdued
envy, yet something

like joy. The ability
to manage life,
even upside-down

embarrasses my feeble
attempts to remain
right-side up.

Sunday Morning Northwest of Austin

A white-winged dove
flutters in the backyard,
lands in a low cedar,
his broad wings flaring,
broad white bands
against dark feathers,
the indiscernible form
of bird and tree now
safe in dark limbs.

Only in low-flight, in landing,
I see bands of white
that mark his feathers,
brand him, distinguished,
for this stark moment.
Otherwise, he seems detached
from a world moving around him,
separate from the very life
that makes him.

A multitude of bird calls
fill morning air,
the first drops of rain,
flowers wanting in mulch.

Silence

I cannot tell you
what I do not understand:

how noise vanishes
when I am alone

the sky folds
like an empty sack

walls become mirrors
no dream can wake.

Kiss the morning sky:
Judas goes to die

alone, unremarkable
except for color

blushing the day –
purple-skinned actor

proud as a king –
his heart, crimson fire.

Only a Crow

Between fading moon
and rising sun
a space of absolute silence.

Only a crow
interrupts.
Empty branches stretch

outward, upward,
straggling, these orbs,
the last twigs

before infinity.
There is no wind.
Nothing moves.

Sound travels so far –
takes me with it,
takes me with it.

Song for Atticus

Like the hummingbird
whose heart beats
ten times a second,
so, your heart rate, now,
is too high to sustain you.

But the hummingbird,
is as mysterious
as it is beautiful –
how does something so tiny
fly so far so fast,
endure so much?

I don't know how long
your heart will beat.
Always life is uncertain
for us all – but I know
you are beautiful.

When I look into your eyes
in your cream-colored face,
even though it is only through
a quarantined camera lens,
already I see something beautiful
and something marvelous –
how the generations combine
in this tiny body in this moment.

Maybe it is my projection,
something I want to see.
But desire is essential to survival.
And that is what I see!

And so, dear boy, I hope
you hear me singing to you
this song of faith
that dares to believe
no matter how many beats
your wings flutter,

already you have made
so many so full of joy.

Despite your difficult start,
the marvel of desire is profound.

The beauty of belief becomes clear

as this evening, in the ancient hills
of Central Texas, for a moment
the clouds open and rays
of patient sun sprinkle
the dripping leaves
after the rain.

Reading *The Odyssey* during the Pandemic

Reading the first great adventure story
of the western world at this time,
sheltered in place, clarifies timeless truth:
The journey is always interior.

Odysseus and I could not be more different.

He is in The Cyclops cave. He dines and dares
with Circe. He sails through treacherous
waters avoiding killer cliffs of his passage.
His men are dying – crying and dying.
Their non-rowing moments are filled
with uncertain feasting and never-ending
rites of prayer and sacrifice to gods
and royalty – receiving gifts
and pledging good will if he survives.

Athena is always near – as is his longing
for Ithaca – his wondering about Penelope
and Telemachus and all that wealth
and privilege he abandoned
just to be a hero.

Oh, if we could redo the past –
those twenty years – are they wasted?
Were they meaningful?
How do they make this moment
of attempted return – this daily journey
of hope and terror, of fear and faith?

All this activity occurs as I sit
in a big blue chair – rowing
through my own past twenty years.

After my morning prayers,
I do laundry, mow the yard, scroll
through Facebook, and once
in a while, journey to the post office
and the grocery store.

Like Odysseus, I have to side-step
strange beings, who may be divine
for all I know. But they seem strange
as I must appear alien to them.

The pandemic ostracizes us all.
We are left with our private returns.
Our journey in solitude, praying
for restoration – to be restored
to what we believe is our rightful place,
our heritage housed in comfortable
freedom – to return to significance,
to community, to family, even Penelope
as we once were. Memories
refusing to die, stubborn with hope.

What has become of everything?
How did Telemachus turn out?
Is Penelope well? Does she miss me?
Has she remarried? How fares Laertes?
Will he die satisfied?

And what of my property? My wealth?
Is it safe? What future awaits me
even if I survive this fated tug-of-war
between man and god, hope and denial?

In my solitude, I am not unlike Odysseus,
after all. I too long to be redeemed.
I too want to put the old days,
the old ways, in renewed perspective.

Still, I can't help but envy the old Greek
traveler. He is forced to think, to scheme.
to act – physical, emotional and mental
action fills his days – orders his moments.
The gods respond to his heart –
even Poseidon whose fierce force
follows him all the way home.

I envy such energy, that motion.
My journey is stationary.
My survival requires patience –
the absurdity of avoiding those I love,
the paralysis of not doing something
foolish – and never quite certain
what that may or may not be.

Sometimes at night, I think I hear Sirens
singing. Can it be for me their chorus
echoes through an empty home?

I often dream of Penelope and imagined
suitors. I wish for competition. Something
to hate, some fellowship of fools to offend.

But the pandemic is sinister.
It foils everything, takes the wind
from my humble sails, makes me
fight my own battles with myself.
The struggle is in me.
Nothing beyond the contested soil
of my soul matters.

Maybe Odysseus figures this out
by the end of his circuitous journey.

He is made by his misadventure.
His longing effects everything –
all he loves, all he values.

On this sunny summer morning
in the big blue chair by the window,
I look out at the eternal journey,
that never-ending sea, so calm
yet so suspect. Endless water
surrounds me, makes me
who I am, who I am to become.

Once again, I pray a pitiful prayer
hoping Athena, and her Zeus,
will guide me, as so many others
through the chilling waters,
across the rugged shores,
past disguised enemies
until I rediscover my soul,
until I return home
to the place I never left.

Nameless

A silent hawk circles
above sumac –
shadows in Cross-timbers.

Sun sets a gilded land,
brown leaves crisping
like unpliable dreams.

I remember a windless day –
Lake Eufala,
like a mirror reflecting

the fall. Already juncos
bunch together
scraping seed in bar ditches.

A young buck, cautious
in his newfound
virility, ducks his head

in a clearing between oak
and red cedar.
Everything I see I need

to know, to understand
all that I love
and all I do not love.

I love what I am not. I love
liberty more
than I hate you. I hate

bondage more than I
love privilege.
So rake your restless leaves.

Validate yourself losing
what little time
you have. Be kind to strangers.

Cut cedar to the roots. Wear sap
for days. Become
something you cannot name.

In Days Before

We would all get together.
The tribe would congregate
around the table. We ate.
We drank. We played games
together. We laughed.
We hunted. We sang
under uncountable stars.

Now we huddle in cells.
I wonder how we remember
those days before – before
we chose alternative allegiances,
embraced alternative realities.
Will truth prevail?
Will we ever be united?

We can never outlive DNA.
We can only change
the societies we enter,
and the cults of our existence
shape us – even to the point
of wishing we were something
we are not.

Not all change is bad, and
of course, change is inevitable.
In our changing, what power
do the days before hold?
Nostalgia is nothing
but a horse-drawn wagon
pulled by ghosts.

The horses have taken flight.
They move on. Maybe we should
as well. But in transitions
such as these, we become
both the whittled stick
and the knife which trims.
Pray for a sharp knife.

Memory can be a curse.
It is a mirror often ignored,
but ignorance does not change
the past, and the future,
like today, dare not
be settled in denial.
Denial is a live volcano.

Eruptions are hard to control.
They force us to our knees.
In lonely isolation
or in remnants of the tribe,
we are playing with fire.
We are betting against
the current of Time.

We are not made to swim
in lava. We cannot
survive that barren stream.
How it all turns out
is anyone's guess.
How it all turns out
is everyone's burden.

Silent Sunday

It is nearly February.
Time moves quietly downstream.
The hassle of the holidays
is behind me now.

I watch finches peck seed
I scattered on the deck,
cigar smoke doesn't seem
to bother them. Gray

clouds determine today,
but hope hovers as well.
The politics of bad Jesus
take a back seat for a bit.

Bare branches host a congregation
of birds – even a few robins,
some jays and a grackle
who is becoming my friend.

His chocolate body, his green
head attract me. He is perfect.
If I were God, I would be proud
to claim him as my own.

There is no traffic this morning.
The world pauses. A breath
of goodness fills my conflicted
lungs. Peace is still possible.

Destiny is never far from my mind,
but destiny, first of all, is
what is – moments that find me
more than what I discover.

A union of thought and repose,
invokes a time to be satisfied
with the small abundance
that invites me to sing.

In this stillness, I am free.
I think of what is essential.
I count the loss as nothing.
I will be, one day, under the dirt

of this clay hillside – particle
in prairie dust, now solidified
in the argentine flora
that engulfs me, even as I breathe.

By Blood Alone

The constructs have all
but fallen, what little
remains are hinged
on guilt and denial.

Like too many American clans,
we throw the horizon
away – excommunicate
dissension.

We prefer morning clouds
for their literal sway,
yet nothing about them
invokes hope of rational thought.

How foreign Jesus really has become.
What a belief we share
with Nazi devils –
children stymied like caged fowl.

We talk of blood. We bleed
for our Lord, as he bled for us.
But no stream flows
from your house to mine.

No avuncular wit, no brother,
no buddies – the patriarch
silent as a lamb at his trough
awaiting talk radio

our current dispensation
of divine revelation – spoiling
for a fight – women
fight, while men duck

and cover, dabbling with duty
misconceived as days-old bread,
dried hard, cracked – something
only grandma's chickens might take.

In the prison of memory
I see what never was,
what never can be –
gathered around the cedar tree

singing carols, a gypsy choir,
good-enough talent
held together by fraying strands
stitched for appearance for a time.

No, we are a farm-yard filled
with abandoned machinery
idly rusting – loitering –
we live by blood alone.

Self-delusion

Who is more culpable:
the one who leads
others to destruction

or the one who follows
a leader
to his demise?

Who are you to think
the violins
play for you?

Too many days,
life is petty betrayal,
self-delusion,

a mockery
to keep the abyss
out of mind –

praying at the pious altar,
trading one insanity
for another.

Walking in Bricktown

She placed her arm into mine
and I became her escort –
I prefer the old-world use
of the word – I am a guide,
a protector – I feel important
and proud – like I am the one
who knows – who names –
but soon I am just a searcher –
too much is unknown.
I look for signs, sniff the air,
see what may be around
the next corner – seeking
myself more than anything

WITH GRATEFUL ADMONITION

One Sandy Night

On the Salt Fork
we staked our rods
baited for catfish,
yellow tips visible
by fire light.

One sandy night
frogs chortled,
something splashed
in the current,
something winged

fluttered about us
in the dark breeze.
Speechless, we
saw heaven's fire
fall – felt the pulse

of the universe
swaddle us
in primal care,
nurtured
with sandy silence.

Morning

Morning is a dream
all its own

when light first appears
when birds first sing
when a breeze first stirs.

You enter false darkness,
a traveler who could never fathom
the timing of your life.

You can only receive it anew,
again, like any other morning

when in the dawning breeze,
you hear the birds
and decide to dance
the silent symphony
that makes you

that turns the world
without notice,
stirring longings
that cannot be ignored.

Leaves of grass,
in any season, yellow or green,
bend with the slightest intention.

Landing

The way a phoebe
or a chickadee
or any delicate winged creature
glides into the thick green
of oak and elm

the marked way they slow
to a precise landing
after accelerating
from a previous post
to their next destination

graces the lower sky,
fills the branches with song,
reminds me how confusing
it can be to be human –
misdirected, lost at home.

Looking across Pasture

Empty except for two pecan trees
still full with green
despite October air,
fescue and johnson, a few
sunflowers fading along the fence.

This soundless scene holds me.
It is not bright enough
for birdsong, no wind –
only space – like a dream
before waking.

Who was the first actor
on this stage?
Does his legacy rest
in the soil, in the air?
Was his elegy ever written?

Maybe

A single scarlet sumac
stands between two fully-green
cedars, round and three times as tall,
beneath cloudless, pale sky,
like the paper I use to record
what I have so often seen.

Sun in far-away eastern horizon
keeps them in shadows,
for the moment, the way dark memory
unexpectedly dawns.

Color, we are told, may only be
the sun's reflective effect.
Nothing intrinsic or essential
abides in those trees that color morning.

Maybe.

I admit no moral could I offer
except to again see
the way a single scarlet sumac
stands between two fully-green
cedars, round and three times as tall.

First Dark

In the southeast sky
it comes first,
a blanket gently drawn,
a bed of comfort
awaiting your entry,
body and soul.

You know it will be darker,
much darker, before long –
and who of us is qualified
to speak of blackest night?

But it is that first dark
that excites me, entices.

I crane my neck toward
endlessness.
I cannot look away.

Southern breeze simmers
with sounds
of seduction.

Now the Night-birds

return –
audition for the part
nothing else can play.

Coyotes have already howled.

Sun and wind are gone.

Dissipation loses sway.
Desire is nothing
even drifting away.

Silence –
a neighbor's dog growls a bit,
a farm truck going home
follows a dark road,
a mooing cow.

Darkness arrives
and now
night-birds, hidden
close enough to touch,
tell their stories

stopping here,
in secluded post oaks –
journeys that never end.

In Reflection

I wait on the moon
to rise through distant trees
in fiery ascent
I have never outgrown.

It is enough
to capture, hold me,
a willing prisoner –
its glowing ordinance

summons to sit tight
in a sagging lawn chair
peering at the top
of trees, drawn beyond

to some horizon
I cannot reach, except
in reflection, some
knowing, churning

while night creatures
hum darkness full,
and stars, in patient
order, fall into place.

Some of That Jazz

I'm not in a club or pub,
not in a concert hall.

I'm isolated on a prairie.
Coltrane's *Love Supreme*

is not everything –
but it's close enough tonight.

Subtle Morning

The subtle morning
shifts before me
so slight, so slow
with uncertain clarity.

Color flashes
in the cedars,
a warbler of some kind
sings atop a brush pile,

his song answered
by unseen bids
in the darker woods.
Stillness surrounds us.

The tremulous sky
hangs with the possibility
of afternoon showers.
Fading grass lingers

in growing daylight.
I am calming
myself – the dew sprinkled
lawn hosting yellow

sunflowers drooping
in September's insistent pull.
Everything is a mirror.
Nothing much

is better than this
quietness before the rush
of day – contentment
filling me,

purifies, I pray, keeps
me. September comes subtly,
a welcome softness
after brusque summer

too long, too oppressive,
too lonely. Change
is at hand. I sense it
in my slowing pulses

an unpretentiousness
pulling me to what I
can only follow, guessing
what only can be felt.

For the Birds, and Other Angels

Speak to me
in the language
of God.

Correct my
faulty vision,
my fearful

ambition
that permits
strife at home,

a countenance
governed too long
by futile

aspiration
to become what
I never should be,

misguided attempts
to hold life
in one hand

while wagging
a finger
with the other.

Winter Juncos

Their wings flutter
for scattered seed.

Evening glows soft
on their shoulders.

They rest a bit,
then flit away

to cedar limbs
in brumal dark.

January Moon

The last moon of January
looks down from its exalted place
high on the western horizon,
blue morning sky, a few white
clouds skirting its first days
of waning. By next week it
will no longer appear round.
Its journey toward darkness
will fulfill its cycle.

If I were that moon I could look
down on this tested land inhabited
by scoundrels who burn books
like "witches" of old – the willfully
ignorant who assume their clamored
"revolution" to make them "great again."

But they have not considered how
they will survive without anointing
a king, making themselves serfs,
once again, lining up to be dross,
automatons serving a market
that chews them up, spits them out
as offal – "The poor always
with us" and other incomplete
mantras they have rarely read
and never understood.

They are baby birds in a nest,
open-mouthed, crying in hunger
for some strange but familiar
force to fill their gullet.

At least parental birds flush
their chicks from the nest –
expect their offspring to fly
on their own – to use those wings
for more than a baby blanket.

That moon! I can't look away!
Pink Floyd's "Comfortably Numb"
resounds in my memory, but I
can't help but imagine that prominent,
omniscient moon knows
how limited, how debilitating
self-imposed numbness finally is.
The guitar riff (not to mention
the creative lyrics, the energetic
vocals), ironically undermines
the very suggestion of numbness.

Though I have my moments,
on this wintry morning, I look up
at a glaring, guilt-invoking moon
and pledge my allegiance
to uncomfortable truth.
I reject numbness that offers itself
so easily to anyone afraid
to face themselves, anyone
unwilling to follow this celestial body
on its journey to darkness.

Monad

My world –
the only world,
nomos itself – landscaped
with fierce, merciful
life that gives

and takes
in symbiotic stewardship.
Erotic energy to breathe –
to bear seed, to die –
recycle.

Never an Eden
except for a few ecstatic moments
grasped – and grasping –
when time hushes,
work and weed recoil.

Flicker

Knocking loud enough
to cause me to look up

from my book and morning coffee,
she drills into a light pole.

I wish she would drop it
to the ground, this artificial

light, so unnecessary,
so oppressive to us

whose eyes have adjusted
to the dark,

who have learned to see
the light of the dark.

By the Light of Fire

Camped in the black of night
beside the White River
submerged in darkness,
only the sounds of water
known, a moving presence,
unceasing, one thing
that makes life, and makes
life bearable – even in the dark.

My tent stands in the silhouette
of flickering flame, something
winged buzzes close by –
fire has that appeal –
two whippoorwills sing
in the hardwoods.

Sleep is hard to find these days.
Night sky fills with the past
looming – stars, above all,
are symbols of the eternal present,
those facts that always are,
secrets we carry in our skin,
and like skin, changes
are so unnoticed, we hardly feel
anything but the same.

The body is an old stage
where humble players have tried
their futile best to remember
lines to dramatize what everyone
has sometimes realized,
that which we allow, from time
to time, to be realized.

Listen. Listen again to that old
song – the verses are for you.
They are about you. You
are an instrument, ordained
by the universe to receive this tune.
Let it carry you downstream,
along the turning, against
the rocks – the undeniable flow.

Paschal Moon: Dawn

At the lake, the moon floats
in the west – a giant light
hanging in lingering dark.
Turkeys gobble leaving the roost.
Coyotes in the distance,
hundreds of songbirds
fill first rays of sun.

Barely a breeze – water
glistens like glass – an orange bobber
suspended above white marabou jigs –
thoughts of a grandson
who will one day fish here,
memories of a son – me
in my eternal childhood –
catching crappie – nothing stirs
except a couple of wild ducks
cutting a wake through stillness,
surface carp splashing.

Today is Palm Sunday
and everything feels right
for the moment – praise
seems appropriate – a natural
voice calling from the depths
of what you want to believe
is soul – an innate desire
to trust, to hope, to care.

You know the vile acts
of humanity are close at hand,
but for now, you see
cormorants circling overhead,
now you put away the crassness
of anything human, anything
that corrupts this vision.

You know this holy day
portends this holy week – things
we call holy, born in betrayal,
refusal to reform – contention
for control, corrupt power.

Whose turn is it now?
Same as those gone before.

Maundy Thursday awaits –
that dark night, sweating blood
in a garden – that false justice
arrested in deep night – then
that misnamed Good Friday –
surely an act of faith –
when torture poses as order,
some disturbed legality.

Oh sure, you want resurrection.
Don't we all?
But that is yet a week away.
Bloody forsaking comes first.

But today, in this early light
a scissortail on a limb faces west
where the moon has gone.
New sun on her shoulders,
soft gray head, sharp eyes,
peppered tail, salmon belly
filled with the heart of Christ.
She returns again
and again, to this place
I come every year
just to worship –
yes, that's the only word
that feels right.

Cardinal: July 4th

It's a sunny Sunday morning,
a Cardinal perched
at the top of a green elm
sings "America the Beautiful"

no triumphant military marches,
nothing sentimental,
no false nostalgia
for an imagined time
that never was – should never be –
no "America First" ideology

just beauty sung humbly,
poetically, somewhere
in a backyard in America
on a sunny Sunday morning

the real Independence –
freedom's truth –
liberty and justice - and beauty
for everyone

anyone patient enough to listen
to birds sing
with grateful admonition.

AN ACHE DEEPER THAN BONE

The Uneven Landscape of Love

It would be wrong to call her an angel,
to dismiss too easily her human kindness,
the choices she embodies to care
for a clumsy fool, to try to smooth
what may be smoothed, and still caress
the rough – the uneven landscape
of love – that makes life interesting,
if not something more.

I don't know of any angel who gives
her body as sacrament, her flesh
gleaming like sunset, yet never
giving way to darkness.

Her breath is morning breeze.
Cottonwood leaves tingle
at her touch – as God's own self
washes over me when she leans close,
head turned to hear the music
of birds through an open window,
holding me spellbound
with the purity of childhood.

Strands of hair flowing down
transfer beauty – like a hawk softly
coming to rest on a decaying limb
in sage-filled desert dust
where everything matters.

Clouds at Dusk

in ambient light
float my way,
pushed by a pleasant breeze,
help me forget the heat
of a day too long, sun
too bright, air
too thick.

I take my place
under the moving sky,
draw a deep breath –
feel brief satisfaction

but then look up again
into layers of purple blue
circling above –
notice brims of darkness
filling the sky,
filling me.

Preference

Like Berryman seeking restoration,
we are too easily beset – not sin,
so much, but awareness that grace
abounds all the more …

                         leaf tips
on a lilac bush mauled by yellow
grasshoppers, shameless in plunder,
as if green is sin to be devoured –
defying symptoms, preferring disease.

Ladybug

One of those days to avoid
if you could see it coming – questions
hammering bent and slippery nails:
Ladybug crawling on the ceiling,
do you know you are upside down?

I am bound to the familiar.
Whispering friends (like trees and grass)
guess something is wrong with me –
I won't fight you on that, but what?

The answers amount to the same
thing – my failure to see –
honest deception lying somehow
in tall grass – like despair.

I Think of Her

once in a while –
that killer smile,
that fragile, wounded life –
a wife, a criminal,
yet ever a child.

Obeying impulses
she never learned –
that ironic honesty of self,
lost on her –

in constant buzz
never knowing the solace
of a hive –
all that honey wasted
in thin air.

Playing the Blues

He plays to keep away the blues.

He plays blue to keep blue
from taking him down to a place
he knows is waiting – bad
moon draped in dark cloth –
cold, obscure, but certain.

I feel it too – fingers bouncing
guitar strings, sad prancing –
blue fog covering us.

Lean in – look close
at the hands – hands that move
up and down frets – at first
by forlorn will, giving over
now to something comfortable.

I look to his hands to save us,
to keep us from nothing,
from the cold, blue nothing.

The Nurture of Trees

Life unfolds
like a sleeveless shirt
strewn across the bureau
where a mother blinks
into her mask, ignores
the stomach growls
of the family cur
that knows more than we
about managing blood
and thunder.

Gold fish in murky bowls
circle with a mania
indistinguishable.
Cell-phoned children
enter darkness, lost
like stray cats – song-less
but savvy and surreal –
surviving with no memory
of a cross, or even
the nurture of trees.

Balloon

A balloon drifting
above the crowd fades
toward that point
no eye can see.

What we think we believe
prompts us to walk
away, a child
deflated, holding string …

What We Forget

Men are turbid roses
drowning in bunches of idiocy.

Their women fill their lungs
with petulance, then stumble
in drunken blindness
but call it courage – slurring
words, sounding like a rabbit
in the jaws of a coyote –
the shrill death-note pierces
everything sacred.

It lasts only a minute,
but it lasts far too long.

Flowers are for funerals
and only ghouls
like death, especially when
trying to replace one
vain cause with another.

Masculinity flowers
in a hot house, petals
droop at random.
Nothing but thorns
outlast withered betrayal

and too many, too soon,
forget too much.

Llewyn Davis Says

There are two kinds of people:
Those who divide the world
into two kinds of people,
and ...

"Losers?" – Jean interrupts him,
abruptly finishing
his intended contrast.

I think they both may be right.

I think I drift between the categories,
and I think whichever category
I am in at any given moment
depends on more than each
of us knows about ourselves

and I think that overthinking
and underthinking, both
cost way too much –
bargains we cannot afford.

Between Us

Looking up
I wonder about you –
I wonder about you and me.

The stars seem so close together,
as if we could just skip
from one brightness to the next

and never worry about falling
into that dark eternity
between us.

Returning

Of all the lovers I never had,
you excite me most:

a bright rare bird
returning –

from the topmost branches
looking down

at sparrows who never left
peck the grass.

Possessed

3 am – alone in total silence,
I sip coffee and drift
between stupor
and marvel

at the full white moon
possessing everything,
even creeping
into the house

where, on a couch, I languish
like one stoned
on black coffee
and white moon beams.

Almost incapacitated,
as if incarcerated –
barely able to feel time
ticking by – a thought

here and there emerges
but disappears
like darkness engulfed
in scarlet streams

of inescapable moonglow
too white
to evade, too fierce
to appease.

Syntax

How do you grieve a question mark?

The love you believed changed shape
like summer clouds pushed

      by southern wind

           and joggers trot by

silly in their costumes all serious
about immortality

as if a sentence always ends
                   with finality.

Lonely Texas at Dusk

Through cedar hills
the road spins like a top
spun by some force
I cannot reckon –
momentum spinning me
around, through me,
the whole world
twirling.

Yet as I turn with dusky eve,
I smell glimpses of juniper,
see blue and orange and yellow
flowers in the periphery
of today – limestone
flowing with spring run-off

and I try to tell myself
that things will turn
out right, someday.
If I can just navigate these turns,
I will find welcome
and I will rest
beside a live oak
beneath a surprising new
Texas moon.

Climbing Rimrock Trail

the way up and the way down
are one and the same
                    — Heraclitus

Something about the name
attracts me, something
about the sheer outcropping,
the face on the edge,
a mirror to the vulnerable.

Despite the bright morning,
something welcomes me
into a fellowship of loss,
a harsh friend telling
me I'm not the only fool
falling for false beauty.

I am surprised how quickly
I move up the rocky trail,
breathing as if I'm used to this,
like I'm sprinting upward
to get away from something
below that pursues me,
pushing me upward.

At the summit, I feel the lowest,
while I pause a few seconds
on the brink of things, look out,
look down, look back
and know I can't stay here.

In Desert Dust, a Flower

Maybe it's for the best I don't even know
    a name, what or how to call you.

I see the curious dance of light
    fresh on stems, bright and new.

A listless breeze conjures memories
    which give way to mysteries.

There is no border here, nothing more
    to restrain, no two sides,

no right, no wrong – just the dust
    around us – and a flower, for all its worth.

Reading Wendell Berry

Morning sun seeping in,
coffee on the stove,
we read Wendell Berry
to each other in bed.
I am dazed that she knows
his work. I can't believe
I am experiencing this.

We are moths in Kentucky
hardwoods, carried on a breeze
that whispered all night
through the grassy dark –
now exposed, unguarded,
but expectant – dew dripping
and drying – as it will.

Moonlight on Snow

Night gathers slowly,
almost without notice,
but some dark never
fills the void. Somber
moon-glow shines
across a pensive expanse,
and you surrender
to quiet that kills more
than it knows – longing
like love, an ache
deeper than bone.

THE DUST TO WHICH WE ALL RETURN

Rainy Morning: Memorial Day, 2021

I'm glad the drops are gentle.
Enough violence has already fallen.
A good death is what most desire.
To be remembered is obliged grace.
Memories falling from the sky
of history, like morning rain,
ping the back deck – each sound
a life I recall – each sound,
someone's life someone knew.
Individual drops fall together.
Death is the ultimate democracy.
Morning rain, like death, a returning
reminder, how we should live.

Breathing the San Juan Mountains

I try to climb but my lungs tighten,
anxiety rises. I scramble up
from a stream hidden deep in a ravine,
too steep for this old goat.
Heavy breaths bludgeon my lungs,
hammer my heart.
I'm a pale trout gasping.

On my knees, I finally reach a plateau.
I drop my rod, my pack –
I'm sure I'm about to faint.
I wonder if this is the place I die.

I wobble off my knees, hunch upright,
remove my broad fishing hat,
hold it tight to my face,
blow into its sweaty cavity,
gulp returning oxygen – this process
slowly resuscitating my grateful gills.

When the panic has passed,
I reflect on the power of recycled breath.
I take in the marvelous wilderness,
think this would be a good place to die –
but how much better to survive.

Face Time from Paris

A miracle of technology
allows me to see their faces
street-side in front of *Notre Dame,*
which is scaffold for repair.

They appear so close, but distance
is evident – technology's magic
brings us together by framing distance,
exploiting emotion with images –
like gargoyles – both practical
and cultic.

Even this indomitable edifice
is not immune from injury.
Its grace, its power seems qualified
somehow – unlit, unopened,
bearing long-lasting wounds.

Will it ever be right again?
Even in repair, some things lose
their original glow – like a marriage,
or even faith itself – after God
has been codified and commodified
for so long we tend to believe
with only half a heart – though we want,
really want to believe, so we make up
feelings, construct ideals, raise
scaffolding around centuries-old belief.

So that on New Year's Eve, tourists
from Texas can eat street-vendor crepes
in freezing weather while calling you
with their device to tell you
how much they love you, wish
Happy New Year – and mean every word,
as if they are present, with you,
touching in a crowded room
or walking arm-in-arm in a frosty field.

Their faces glow with the afternoon light.
The light is always right here I am told.
We've taken tons of pictures.
The light is always right.

Winter Coming Hard

for Paul Austin

I.

Winter will be long.
Winter will be hard.

Uncertainty, withdrawal,
unwelcome change looms.

In mid-Autumn,
we gather, meet friends
and family, feel October sun
masking us.

But we are not sure
how to proceed, how to plan
for the demands
of colder, darker days.

We know this, somehow,
in the subtext of ourselves.
Hallway mirrors reflect
members of a marked humanity.

Always, we hope it will not be so.
Always, we attempt to block scenes
playing our minds.

We resolve ourselves,
once again, to be
as happy as our soul dares.

Determined to endure – not
to give in, we push back
against the psychic burden:

The plague, the presidency,
the denuding of a democracy – the result
of our materialism – an outdated,
self-induced fantasy waltz
of superiority and endless resources
even as we destroy our only home
trying to placate the American Nero,
the coward who projects hollow poison,
a deranged child with access –
who owes the devil – enabled
by the greedy, propped
by paranoia, one-dimensional,
delusional, deceitful lust for power –
a false glory that flirts
with a few minutes of history.

II.

When the ice melts, will we see a true greening?

Will there be reason to go outdoors,
to breathe morning sun waking
dew off flowers?

Will birdsong matter?

How many unattended funerals
will clog our memory?

How many rights will have been erased?

How much treasure will have been wasted?

How much stolen?

What else? What else?

By then, their "revolt" will be dust
or in high gear – but it makes little differences
at this moment.

Already we have had too much insult,
too much injustice. One violation
of personal liberty is one too many.

We will survive,
something tells me,
but what we will be
remains a matter of faith.

A Mother's Grave

Years of anger drift away
like topsoil in the wind.
Only deepest roots remain
under rocks refusing to budge.

Memory is too elastic to hold tight.
We must stretch with what binds us.

Once I thought it would break,
would not hold – despite my attempts.
I have returned to her,
so tentatively, through the years.

But each return was a new game
played the same old way,
with familiar words – abrupt,
working hard to be gentle

but often failing. Scars cut deep
in the soul – some unseen,
where some could never go.

And that, I tried, long ago, to conclude,
was how it must be – if only I could live
that way, if only I could forget,
if only I could re-create the past,
and if not, make something new, now,
for the time being. Time remaining.

Standing here – head bowed, eyes
discerning, disconcerted – half-aware
of summer breeze in the leaves,
it occurs to me that early summer
(or is it late spring?) is the best time
for her to go.

Winter was always too rough.
Too many holidays. Too much loneliness.
Too many jagged memories
that would never completely smooth.

Too many puzzles missing too many pieces.

But in warmer weather,
when flowers bud, when birds sing,
she came to life again – reached
some weird equinox

her children felt, with beleaguered
calm, despite storm warnings
that kept her up nights.

This fluctuation became her rhythm
(maybe it was always so). Storm clouds,
the crash of thunder, a downpour,
but the clear sunrise in the morning.

The rising sun, warm and forgiving,
a comfort she relied on,
a pattern of destruction, never fully
realized – a sordid redemption
that overcame her apocalyptic neurosis.

A sunny morning – revived – an abandoned
childhood momentarily reclaimed,
when the flowers of her best self, continue

and a family, bowed with uncertainty,
regard her mixture of faith and fear –
and in the end, admit something too painful
to ignore, too mysterious to explain.

Grave stones have dark appeal.
They tend to endure – age with vicissitudes,
vacillate with veritable claim.
Changeless midst the change,
they stand for something always alive,
always hopeful, always present.

Finally, there is nothing to be said.
Death, like life, floats away.
Children feel this early, even if they
can't realize its full effect.

Graves remember.
With gracious imperfection,
Grave stones remind us.

Uriel's Visitation

The builder knows what he has built can't last
forever, but to watch it burn before his eyes
singes his soul, never to recover.

The house, built with his hands, designed
with shelves just the right height for her,
with two sinks and rooms for grandkids,
a place to know who you are,
where you come from – gone.

Men and boys in yesterday's barn listening
to the engine of the restored tractor turn over,
purr like grandma's cats – gone.

All the labor, all the pleasure, all the purpose
of this place consumed to ash –
a bird feeder, charred, standing alone,
relic to some apocalyptic sword
slicing the flesh of Christ,
eviscerating the blessed community
trying to stand on its knees –
an unquenchable oracle.

An Evening in Spring

It was a fine spring evening
somewhere in western Oklahoma.
We were building a pole barn.
I was on leave from college, working
with dad and my uncles – wheat
and cattle country for miles.

It was a pleasant drive home.
My tired muscles flexing, a feeling
of virility, of belonging.

Uncle Max talked the most, told stories,
recounted history – our family philosopher.

A grain elevator came into view.
Pickups and a couple of tractors crowded the lot,
an ambulance and lights of a sheriff's car.

We stopped – this fine spring evening – to see.
An elevator had exploded, dumping tons
of grain, burying a driver in his truck.

All we could see was a mountain of wheat,
golden as sun this spring evening.
Word funneled to us – yes it was true.

A tractor with a front-end loader and men
with scoop shovels began the delicate task
of excavating, shoveling through the mound.

All was silent except the drone of a tractor engine,
the occasional squawk of the sheriff's radio.

There was nothing to be done. After a while
we drove away in our own silence,
feeling life more tenuous than harvest.

A few miles down the road, Uncle Max spoke:
It's just one of those things.
Just one of those things.

When it's your time to go, there's nothing you can do.

More silence – maybe a nod of heads.

When it's your time to go, it's your time to go.
That's all there is to it.

On this spring evening, only wind rushing
through open windows now seemed to matter,
the tentative sun setting among us.

The Bridge

for Mike Thompson
In Memoriam

How often we talked
with passion long
into the night,
darkness raging
around us.

Listening – our voices
clinging to what faith
we could find,
what hope remained,
remembering joy.

What metaphor best
defines you? Our
times together?
A light, a warm fire,
a strong, gentle hand?

Our voices speaking,
seeking to understand
the symbols of life,
the signs of society,
reassuring goodness.

From the known
to the unknown, and back
again – determined
to discover, to uncover
paths of truth

we walked with careful
diligence, committed
to our imperfect
rhythms – brothers
for this short life.

You bridged the abyss,
chasms of mortality,
making a way possible.
And now, as always,

I hear you calling:

This is the way.
Follow me brother.
We'll get there.
Trust the bridge.
Follow me brother.

Blue Jay

The Elm is leafless.
A Jay lands
on a bare branch,
screeches.

Is he angry?
Disappointed?

Why can he not sing,
or is his song
a protest, lacking melody,
but worth the hearing?

Kids in Cages

I write my deep anger.
I feel helpless, feel my voice
dying, a pitiful chirp
in a lost canyon.

Kids are in cages
in US custody
so our border can be safe!

I think the powers know
if they just ignore us
eventually our voices
will simply fade,
the way a rushing wind
first startles, then lessens
in our hearing.

The wind howls its insult
but we allow it to blow away.
Our ears, our souls – like locks
on a cage – close.

So we wait in stupor
for the next outrage to tap us
on the shoulder – stir us –
some new breeze
on which we may temporarily
fly our hapless, helpless
democratic kite.

Even a Child

Children make up stories.
Wise people listen close.

It takes courage to find the child in you.

Even the most vulnerable self
is worthy of recognition.

These are their stories:
Tree houses where goblins cannot go.
Yellow school buses
with black puppies waiting.

The evening star is a friend
until supper is called
and the belief in something beyond
is substituted by macaroni and cheese.

After dinner, it is time for lessons in hate,
subjects that keep democracy
in tumult – because daddy says so,
because daddy was told so
by some hired gun in a box –
somebody who long ago
climbed down from his tree house,
forgot to wish on the guiding star,
now is taken over by hate
because there is no cause
like "the lost cause" –
no pride like paranoia.

The coward wears his red badge –
something even a child
could not imagine.

The Red Mud of Home

The red mud of home
is losing its claim
though I can never
cleanse its stain.

When you benefit
from a lie,
it is always easy
to believe other lies

until you are stuck
in the muck
you call truth –
mistaking nostalgia

misusing terms like
heritage, family,
faith, freedom –
making yourself a victim

with nothing to do
but blame abstractions,
churning nonsense
like grandma's butter.

Betrayal is the prime
act of the deluded,
and delusion is the cost
of dishonest indulgence.

No god can turn
willful stupidity
into virtue – call it
what you will.

Tribute to John Lewis (1940 -2020)

His face always spoke sincerity.
But I have seen something else, too.
Beneath the sad enduring lines,
beyond his fierce, worried eyes,
a kindness remained,
a gentleness born of sacrifice,
a disposition that made the fire
burn – not only hot,
not only righteous –
but also, may we always remember,
with welcome.

Snake Bit: A Moral, Political Fable

You know the old joke
born of legend:

When a snake bites you,
find someone to cut
the assaulted flesh,
and suck out the poison.

The great question:
What if the snake bites you
on the ass?

The ironic, visceral answer:
That's how you know
who your real friends are.

It Will Hold

Inside the Statue of Liberty
photos and quotes document
the process of making,
delivering and erecting
this grandest of symbols.

One quote has stayed with me:
"It will hold" written in response
to those who worried
the statue, as designed, might not
withstand weather, were it erected
in the harbor, unprotected.

Time has proven the strength,
the durability of the design.

Standing in that hallowed space,
I marveled at the engineering,
but soon I also sensed
an intrinsic symbolism –
will Democracy hold?

I have often contemplated
that symbolic phrase – reviewing
our fragile history, as well as
current political, social challenges.
Will Democracy hold?

I confess, at times I worry,
but when I look more closely,
I am heartened. When I see
the continued grace and courage
of our Black brothers and sisters,
when I hear the continuous chorus
of so many of every ethnicity,
of every denomination, and
especially the wisdom of our youth,
hope returns – It will hold!

It will hold despite the terror
of white racists. It will hold
despite the slimy traitor-ship
of right-wing politicians,
the malicious, opportunistic
contortions by public servants,
by Evangelicals wielding
self-righteous slogans
marked by selective listening
masked in faithless fear,
contributing to a swollen river
of hate – foolish cravings
for a theocracy.

But, it will hold!

It will hold as long as you and I
want it to hold.
Every word that counters a lie,
every act that clarifies
misconception, that confers
liberty and human dignity for all,
keeps the dream upright.

We hold "these truths
to be self-evident" and what we
hold, holds Democracy,
makes everything possible
for all of us.

It will hold.

Reflections: July 4, 2021

We need an Interdependence Day!

Independence was once a calling
and we have heard its tune,
have followed its score
to its inevitable conclusion.

Now we must celebrate Interdependence.

American indulgence will kill us.
We will become extinct
unless we change – sing a new song –
and the extinction will not be
an Armageddon-type
catastrophe that takes us out
in a blaze of glory.

The process of becoming extinct
is a slow, but sure, devaluation
of self and society –

a draining of aquifers,
demolition of hardwoods,
invasion of misplaced botany,
death to multitudes of species,
one by one – a solastalgia
so seductive we hardly notice,
especially if we are hyped
on nationalism.

We must resist domination.
We must join the intricacies
of all life – be part
of the ecosystems
that would sustain us
if only we would share

if only we would be stewards
of the wilderness we inhabit,
husband our gardens
responsibly, collectively,
intelligently ...

Land of the free / Home of the brave –
sure, but only

when we are at home
with the planet
at home with the honeybees,
with the whales,
the songbirds,
the reptiles

the desert and the sea,
the moon and the stars

the dust
to which we all return.

About the Author

Much of Ken Hada's poetry is formed on his back deck in rural Pottawatomie County, Oklahoma. His work has been awarded by The Western Writers of America, The National Western Heritage Museum, SCMLA and The Oklahoma Center for the Book. He has also been featured on *The Writer's Almanac* and other digital formats. Ken directs the annual Scissortail Creative Writing Festival at East Central University in Ada, Oklahoma. He enjoys traveling to meet with folks, give public readings and workshops. Contact and other information is available at: kenhada.org. *Contour Feathers* is his ninth poetry collection.

CPSIA information can be obtained
at www.ICGtesting.com
Printed in the USA.
LVHW092017240921
698682LV00002B/185

9 781735 576244